IN THE STREETS OF TEHRAN

Woman. Life. Freedom.

by Nila

translated from Persian by Poupeh Missaghi
with an introduction by Christina Lamb

ITHAKA

First published in the UK by Ithaka Press
An imprint of Black & White Publishing Group
A Bonnier Books UK company

4th Floor, Victoria House,
Bloomsbury Square,
London, WC1B 4DA

Owned by Bonnier Books
Sveavägen 56, Stockholm, Sweden

Hardback – 978-1-80418-452-3
Ebook – 978-1-80418-488-2

A CIP catalogue of this book is available from the British Library.

Typeset by IDSUK (Data Connection) Ltd
Printed and bound by Clays Ltd, Elcograf S.p.A

1 3 5 7 9 10 8 6 4 2

Ithaka Press is an imprint of Bonnier Books UK
www.bonnierbooks.co.uk

for my country, Iran

Introduction

Month after month they came out into the streets of Iran. '*Zan, Zendegi, Azadi!*' they chanted – 'Woman, Life, Freedom!' Leading the way were students and teenagers, mostly female, their courage astonishing.

Throughout late 2022 and on into 2023, like many around the world I followed transfixed. Every morning from afar I checked Telegram and other social media channels, half excited and awed by the women's bravery, and half terrified of what the response to them would be from one of the most vicious regimes on earth.

The regime retaliated with arrests, killings, rape, and by blinding them with shot from paintball guns. Yet even after the executions started, still the women continued to protest.

One woman, right after being released from detention, stood in front of the prison gate and shouted slogans against Supreme Leader Ayatollah Khamenei until she was arrested again.

It was, it seemed, the first ever women's revolution.

*   *   *

Perhaps no image captures the mood better than that of a young woman standing on a car roof, hair uncovered, hands outstretched as if beseeching the sky, as all around thousands of people walk or drive along the road. They are heading toward the grave of Mahsa Amini, known to family and friends as Jina, a 22-year-old Kurdish woman whose death in the custody of Iran's morality police triggered the uprising.

In September 2022 Mahsa-Jina had gone to Tehran to spend a few days with her brother to celebrate her twenty-third birthday, before heading off to law school. On Tuesday 13 September, as she emerged from a metro station, she was picked up by the *Gasht-e-Ershad,* or morality police, for 'bad hijab' – her hair was apparently showing from under her scarf.

As she was bundled into the white and green van to be driven to a re-education centre, she protested, fearing her holiday would be ruined. According to other women taken, the guards beat her brutally. When they got to the centre, she fainted and was taken to Kasra hospital.

Photographs of her in a coma, with bruises on her arms and tubes emerging from her face, were smuggled out and went viral. People started gathering outside the hospital. By the Friday she was dead, never to see her twenty-third birthday.

The regime's claims that she had a heart attack or collapsed in a diabetic coma were dismissed by her family and friends, who said she was very fit. Photos from the hospital showed a brain injury consistent with blows to her head.

Iranian women are only too familiar with the methods of the morality police. The crowds swelled. 'We all felt it could have been any of us,' said a friend of mine named Anna, a sports teacher and mother of two in Tehran. 'I had friends staying from the south and it could easily have happened to them.'

Mahsa-Jina's funeral that Saturday in her hometown of Saqqez was attended by thousands of fellow Kurds shouting 'Death to the dictator!' Her mother prostrated herself over her tombstone, a portrait of grief. On it were inscribed the words: 'Jina, dear! You will not die. Your name will become a symbol'

It was true. Her name would soon become the most tweeted hashtag in history. Women and girls took to the streets, chanting 'Woman, Life, Freedom!' They tore off their hijabs and made bonfires of them on the streets. Some cut their hair publicly as a sign of mourning. Schoolgirls filmed themselves putting their middle fingers up to the omnipresent photos of Ayatollah Khamenei, the 80-year-old head of Iran's ageing theocratic regime.

In no other country, except under the Taliban in Afghanistan, is it mandatory for women to wear a hijab that covers their entire bodies, allowing only face and hands to show. Many women participated in the 1979 Islamic Revolution to topple the Shah, only to later find themselves being threatened for doing something they had done for years – leaving their hair uncovered. By 1983 going without a hijab had been criminalised and the law was being enforced by armed men who patrolled the streets, the newly formed Islamic Revolutionary Guard Corps (IRGC).

Yet behind closed doors Iranian women dressed very differently, as I discovered on several visits to Iran over the last 20 years. I will never forget turning up at an artist's party in northern Tehran in my long coat and trousers, only to find all the women there in short skirts and skyscraper heels. There was also a well-stocked bar and pounding music – this in a land where any form of nightlife has been banned since 1979, and alcohol consumption is punishable with lashes.

Over two decades I saw this resistance grow bolder. Women began to wear tighter and tighter manteaus or long coats, and colourful scarfs that sometimes slid so far back that they barely wafted over the hair. A few years ago in Tehran I was taken to underground fashion shows, while on a Facebook page called 'Stealthy Freedoms', women posted pictures of themselves doing things like driving without hijabs, skiing or surfing. Transgression was not limited to women: even a policeman in Isfahan whose excellent English I commented on explained he watched American movies using VPNs to circumvent the restrictions. But recent public protests go far beyond these private acts of defiance. Mahsa-Jina Amini's death seems to have opened a floodgate.

It is not the first time Iranians have come out on the streets. In 2009 the so-called Green Revolution took place, months of actions against what citizens saw as rigged elections to install Mahmoud Ahmadinejad as President. The winter of 2019 also saw protests against a hike in fuel prices in what is now known as Bloody November. Each time, demonstrations were brutally suppressed.

Nor was it the first time women had resisted the hijab. In December 2017 a 32-year-old woman called Vida Movahed left her child at home, climbed up onto a utility box in busy Enqelab (Revolution) Street in central Tehran and removed her hijab, tying it to a stick and waving it above her head. Though she was arrested, a number of other women did the same over the next few months.

This time, however, the uprising was massive, having spread to 139 cities and every province. Protesters came from all religions and ethnicities, including not just the Kurdish minority to which Mahsa-Jina Amini belonged, but also Arab, Baluch and Azeri groups, who resent discrimination; the clandestine LGBT community; and all social classes. Oil refinery workers went on strike. TV and film stars joined in, as did top sportswomen, removing their hijabs in international contests in solidarity. Chess master Sara Khadem competed without her hijab, and was forced into exile.

Most of these were Generation Z – Iran has a young population and 60 per cent of its 89 million citizens are under 30. But when daughters went to protests and never came home, with the authorities claiming they had 'fallen off roofs', their mothers were the next to join in.

The movement even has a song, '*Bayare*', which in Persian means 'For' or 'Because of ...', a haunting ballad listing the many ignominies suffered by Iran's people. It was performed by Shervin Hajipour, one of Iran's most famous singers, who soon found himself arrested.

The protests are of course about far more than a piece of cloth. Those who tell you what to wear will also tell you what to think. Woman after woman told me they have had enough of being second-class citizens whose testimony is worth half that of a man, of having no freedom to travel, of being considered inferior to the husbands or fathers who are their legal guardians.

And though the protests were triggered by the hijab, and the lack of freedom it symbolised, they have drawn in others angered by the regime's mishandling of the economy and the Covid pandemic, which saw Iran suffer one of the world's highest death tolls. Inflation of 50 per cent and the depreciation of the rial to record lows have left many unable to afford rent or meat, despite their country having one of the world's largest oil reserves. More than a million graduates are unemployed. Much of the activists' frustration is over corruption and how much of the economy is controlled by the powerful IRGC.

The demonstrations quickly became the biggest uprising since the 1979 Revolution, the greatest threat to the regime's existence that it has ever faced. And women are at the forefront.

* * *

Who are these brave women who risk their lives day after day and shout slogans night after night? What gives them courage? The Iranian regime sadly refused to let Western journalists into the country to report on the protests. But some women have risked their lives – and navigated internet closures and the monitoring of social media – to get their story out.

Among them is Nila, author of this book. For her protection, we as readers can't know much about her. We know she is older than many of the protesters, having been born during the Iran–Iraq war of 1980–88. Her first memory is of Iraqi planes bombing her home city of Tehran, and the constant blackouts that resulted.

'To write is to testify,' she says, 'to dig deep wells,' and she has done that here. In this short, powerful tract, she conveys the trajectory of the protests, starting with the excitement of what she calls 'a showdown with the patriarchy' where hair becomes 'combat attire' and burning hijabs stand in for Molotov cocktails.

'We are no longer the world's shorthand for misery,' she writes proudly of Iranian women. 'We are the image of resistance.'

With Nila we live the ups and downs of the struggle, seeing dreamlike scenes of 'turban tipping', when students film each other knocking the turbans of clerics, and the day Hijab Street is transformed into No Hijab Street.

Like Persian miniaturists of the past, she captures the smallest details – the people crying silently in shops or doctors' waiting rooms, the lines of riot police sitting on street corners, nonchalantly draining cans of Coca-Cola as they tuck into takeaway cartons.

She also describes the guilt of women of her generation and that of her parents, for the years in which they did not rise up against being forced to live as second-class citizens, when their resistance was confined to an underground life of partying or cursing the ayatollahs behind closed doors.

For Nila, what is happening on the streets can be seen as a psychological revolution. Mahsa-Jina's murder has 'opened our eyes, uniting us in understanding a collective tragedy' and finally overridden the survival mechanisms that have kept so many from speaking out until now.

Iran is a land of poetry, and Nila interweaves her own experiences with some of the country's history and literature, from Ferdowsi's *Book of Kings* to the story of Tahereh, a 19th century poet, revolutionary scholar and women's rights activist, as well as a member of the Babist sect. Married at 13 to a mullah, she refused to accept the norms of society and became a fugitive. Addressing a public meeting, she removed her veil, so shocking her audience that some men apparently slit their own throats. In 1852 when she was just 35, the King had her executed, and her body was thrown into a well above which the National Bank of Iran now stands.

Just like Tahereh, the protesters of today are not unaware of the fate awaiting them. All too often, they are faced with gangs of motorcyclists in their black masks, batons ready to strike.

The crackdown has been brutal. Approximately 22,000 protesters were detained, many in the notorious Evin Prison. Some have been raped in detention. More than 500 have been killed, of whom 50 are children. Many more have been injured, and doctors and nurses are frequently warned not to treat them – though many bravely do. Seven protesters have been convicted of 'crimes against God' and executed. Schoolgirls have ended up in hospital after mysterious mass poisonings. The government even forces the parents of its victims to pay to retrieve their bodies.

A particularly cruel method the regime uses to flush out protesters involves shooting hundreds in the eyes with pellet guns, forcing them to go to hospital, where they are only treated if they sign confessions. Many have been blinded, including a 6-year-old girl who had been playing on her balcony.

'Our Achilles heel,' writes Nila, is that '[o]ur rage is so much greater than our logic.' In the streets of Tehran, she must literally walk through the blood of her fellow protestors. Their anger is enough to threaten and infuriate the regime but not to destroy it – yet.

But in Nila's words we see the strength of these women, and know it is not over. Revolutions are not easy, and this is a marathon, not a sprint.

Among those watching mesmerised from afar was Azam Jangravi, one of the so-called Girls from Revolution Street, who paved the way for today's movement with their own protests in 2017–18. When she stood on a utility box in central Tehran, she says she was terrified but felt like 'the most powerful woman in the world'.

She was not only detained but lost her job, her driving licence and even faced losing custody of her young daughter. The pair fled the country and settled in Canada, where Azam works as a cybersecurity analyst and has helped some of the current protesters escape.

'Seeing all the women coming out after Mahsa's killing, I cried a lot and felt proud,' she told me.

'We face a dictatorial regime. You can't change in one or two years something Iranian women have been fighting for 40 years,' she added. 'But now I'm optimistic. Because when I started I was alone. But right now, the women of Iran are not alone.'

Nila is one of many women still refusing to wear the hijab, declaring 'there is no way that we are going back to how we lived before'.

In an attempt to deter them, in April 2023 the regime launched a 'chastity and hijab campaign', installing thousands of CCTV cameras as part of a mass surveillance scheme that uses facial recognition. Within two months more than a million women had received text messages disciplining them for walking or driving without hijabs.

But the women of Iran will not be deterred. Billboards promoting the campaign continue to be set alight, anti-regime graffiti appears, and at night women scream slogans from the rooftops into the darkness, even as the regime marks the doors of transgressors.

Nila believes all this bravery may be the material for some future equivalent of the fabled *Book of Kings*. Perhaps a *Book of Queens*? I leave you with her words: 'All our thousand-year wars have been nothing but a long prelude to a book containing only this one sentence: women will take back agency over their bodies.'

Christina Lamb

I often leave the house while it's still light outside, around three or four in the afternoon. Outside, the atmosphere feels like the moment before the alarm clock goes off. Inside, the shadows of a huge Monstera Deliciosa's leaves fall diagonally on the floor of my house. The anxious light of autumn draws crooked silhouettes on the walls, angled towards the door. Even the shadows want to leave.

I do not wear my manteau,[1] just a light jacket, black trousers and, even more important than my facemask, my trainers, so that I can run if needed. I'm 'a cloud in trousers'.[2] I close the front door behind me. Immediately, as if I have turned a page in a book, I am in the next chapter. In the streets. And it's here that I look for the destiny of a movement. Look for a revolution. Look for hope.

Why is it that many people like me are being drawn towards the demonstrations? Are we trying to erase what happened during the 1979 Revolution, in the same streets – the protests that ultimately disgorged an Islamic government? Even if, like me, we were not born at the time, we want to repair what was done. We want to purge our national sense of guilt, which we call our 'ignorance', our 'foolishness' or even our 'drunkenness'.

1

Unlike previous protests, this time around, it's not just the city centre that is busy. Some other neighbourhoods are lighting up, too, emerging like glimpses of white porcelain at the bottom of a cup of coffee grounds.

But most days, I still choose to head to a boulevard in the city centre. A big waterway, long dried up, used to flow through it, more than a hundred years ago. Unfortunately, bad luck is not just for rivers.

Before the Islamic Revolution of 1979, somewhere in the middle of that boulevard, just in front of the Ministry of Agriculture, there was a statue of two farmers, a man and a woman. It was a work of high Soviet realism, which the snobbish cultural community of the time barely classed as art. It was a communist cliché: a woman in a loose, ankle-length dress, looking happy, hard at work watering produce. The man stood beside her, holding an industrial wheel.

After the Revolution, clerics from the city of Qom ordered that a tarpaulin scarf be thrown over the head of the woman. Not long after, her ankles, too, were covered with the same fabric. Previously, people simply passed by the statue the way they passed by the electricity poles. It was only after these decisions had been made – for the people's own good – that all their attention was suddenly directed towards the woman's ankles. No ethos other than that of a fanatical cleric or a porn site could render something so innocuous so suggestive. Finally, the distraction of this voluptuous phenomenon proved too much. The whole statue was uprooted and moved to Tehran Museum of Contemporary Art.

When I find myself in that boulevard, I think of the statue's symbolism. But, honestly, I do not really remember it at all. No one does. We head there because the boulevard sits at the crossroads of several other protest routes. I walk the grey boulevard, passing through intersections where small garrisons of crackdown police gather. With their offshoots of motorcycles, batons and anti-riot paraphernalia, they form disorderly rows.

I'm reminded of Khomeini's and Khamenei's photographs, hanging unevenly on the walls of schools and offices. It feels as though they have been there forever: a chaotic presentation of a chaotic power.

For a while now, I, like many other women, have stopped pulling up my scarf to cover my hair when I pass by the guards. I know nothing can stop one of the soldiers from raising his gun and targeting my body with rubber bullets. But what is happening here is for the greater public good.

Social movements are formed of everyday choices, as the sociologist Asef Bayat points out in his work on the movements, particularly in the Middle East. Our marches are a daily presence against the forces of crackdown. They surpass the presence of the police forces everywhere, defying their clumsy, artificial mask of power.

Participating requires more bravery during the day than the night: we are a wave of anxious bodies, of fierce heads with our hair free in the wind. This is us, witnessing our time. But we are not only witnesses. We are activists. And, sometimes, we are martyrs.

History will write about women who rose against the repressive virtues of their time. These are the women who have been sentenced to 20 years in prison, whose right to practise law has been revoked for the crime of defending women's rights. They are the mothers who have been imprisoned for seeking justice for their murdered kids. The women who protested the punishment of death by stoning[3] and, in revenge, were repeatedly taken to the gallows for theatrical hangings. The women who protested the punishment of lashing and were sentenced to dozens of lashes. The woman who set her own body on fire in the middle of a square to protest her lack of bodily autonomy. The women who wrote about femicides in morning newspaper columns and were taken into custody while the papers were still on newsstands. The woman who one day left her young child at home, went out into the city streets, climbed a utility box, took her scarf off and turned it into a flag of protest.

Are these acts of testimony? Are they the work of an invisible society of women that appears in global headlines from time to time, before quickly disappearing again? These women are seen only when their actions lead to imprisonment and execution, because the world is looking only to create myths, looking only for names.

But we are unaware of the destiny of dozens or hundreds or thousands of nameless female activists; perhaps we will always remain unaware. Even for the ones we know, only the course of history or the passage of time will reveal the true extent of their roles.

Looking back at the past 44 years, one thing is clear: the number of Iranian women taking a stand keeps rising. And now their struggle – despite being scattered, despite being slow – has unleashed such a powerful wave of civil disobedience that the world has been forced to look.

We are no longer the world's shorthand for misery. We are the image of resistance.

Tahereh

Mystic poet, orator, theologian, heretic or pariah: during her short life, Tahereh – whose name literally translates to 'the pure one' – forever altered the history of Iran.

Tahereh's life started in a garden and ended in a well. But between her family birthplace in Qazvin, where she was born in 1817, and the outskirts of Tehran, where she was buried in 1852, without a tomb worthy of her name, this revolutionary scholar never stopped challenging the limits imposed upon women of her time.

Her father's house had a garden and a large library that helped shape her. Thanks to reading books and receiving a religious education, usually reserved for men, Tahereh developed a fine knowledge of sacred texts and Islamic law, as well as Persian and Arabic literature. Her education planted the seeds of a spiritual quest that animated her whole life.

And so started a succession of different positions: first, her adherence to the Sheikhiyeh movement, a philosophical branch of the twelve-imam Iranian Shiism born in the middle of the 18th century, which insists on the messianic figure of Hazrat-e Mahdi, the hidden imam. Then came her adoration for Babism,[4] another messianic movement that appeared in the middle of the 19th century in Iran.

The only woman among the first disciplines of the Bab, Tahereh preached Babism until she was imprisoned in 1850. She was believed to have helped usher in a new prophet and the advent of a novel religion that opposed traditional Shiism.

Tahereh did not submit, under any circumstances, to be excluded from society in the name of religion. In her poems and speeches,[5] she questioned everything. She even asked why she couldn't be a cleric when she had, for many years, taught Quranic exegeses to men – albeit while hidden behind a curtain.

Married at the age of 13 to her Shiite cousin, she had three children: two sons and one daughter. It is said that her husband once tried to poison her. The ideological warfare between her and her husband's family, which dragged on for years after their divorce, eventually arrived at a Chekhovian denouement. When her ex-father-in-law was assassinated in the middle of a Shiite mosque, all fingers pointed at Tahereh.

This accusation, which remains a point of contention to this day, added to the mystery that surrounded Tahereh. It divides scholars studying her life into different camps: those who say the murder was carried out by her devout Shiite enemies, and those who insist that, while Tahereh might have not given the Babis direct orders to murder her ex-father-in-law, perhaps she hadn't exactly stopped them either.

Either way, fearing for her life, Tahereh became a fugitive. She left her city of Qazvin behind forever. It is impossible to say whether she carried with her *Qoyum al-Asma*, Bab's first book, which she had translated from Arabic to Persian.

After Bab was arrested, his followers, dispersed and uncertain, decided to hold a large public gathering to speak of their religion.[6] It seems that Tahereh was the one to initiate this. She then also came up with a brilliant idea, which she shared with the Babi men: she should be the one to speak out on their behalf. Counting on a 1,400-year-old law that held that a woman had only half the mind of a man, she knew that, unlike them, she could not be executed for the crime of blasphemy, only forced to repent.

When she appeared on stage to give her speech, she was not wearing her hijab. There are two versions of the story: one says that Tahereh only pulled her face covering away, and the other says that she took off both her head and face covering. According to some history books, there were men who cut their own throats upon seeing her.

With her speech and her symbolic gesture, Tahereh clearly announced that the monopoly of Islam had come to an end. But was the freedom she wanted beyond even that offered by Babism?

Long after Tahereh removed her hijab, even the Babis themselves tried to make everyone believe that this had been an accident. This is reminiscent of the forced confessions that air on state TV during our protests.

Today, on TV, in the news and in the streets, we are extensions of Tahereh – extensions of those who, even up to a hundred years ago, had to cover their faces and bodies and be separated from men on the pavements, just as we today are forced to cover ourselves and sit in segregated buses and train carriages.

What is happening right now is not simply an unveiling. It is an uprising against the Islamic dress code that robs women of their agency. It is the largest women's protest in the past 1,400 years.

We are both activists and witnesses.

Perhaps if, 1,400 years ago, Iranians had accepted Islam of their own will, not under duress following the Muslim Arab invasion of their land, they wouldn't clash with it so intensely. No other nation has gamed Islam to the extent Iranians have: Hurufism, the Nuqtavi movement, Shu'ubiyya ... all were tunnels we constructed under the world of Islam in order to pass through or escape it. Fourteen centuries of indulgence, toleration, politeness, hypocrisy.

Unlike many other nations, Iran did not adopt the Arabic language after the Muslim conquest. We hold tight to the Persian language, a flag passed on from one generation to the next, so that we remember we are Iranian before being Muslim. We must derive our identity not from the confront-ation of two nations, but from that of a nationhood with a religion.

From the very beginning, we have been hung up on the lost grandeur of the Persian Empire: Cyrus the Great's Cylinder; Persepolis; Xerxes, Darius, the Persian rulers of old – every majestic piece of our heritage that we were once known for in the West but are not any more. And a large percentage of us, despite having always been Muslim, much prefer to be seen as Persian in the eyes of foreigners.

No one teaches us this, but we, as Iranians, feel that it's only through clasping our ancient documents engraved in rocks that we can overcome a historical inferiority complex and tell the foreigners who we once were. Our obsession goes so far as to erase any critical questioning of the past.

This lack of a critical perspective and this longing for past glory, accompanied by the expansion of Islamic thought, has paved the way for an intensifying patriarchal mindset. And this is the game many of us are not willing to play any more. We have realised that we must cast a critical eye on everything. And that's why, after many centuries of complaisance, the citizens of this country are in a showdown with patriarchy.

This, perhaps, is the zenith of the Woman, Life, Freedom movement. Yes, the patriarchy we are fighting against is closely tied to religion enforced by a specific regime, but its roots burrow so deeply all around the world that our struggles are tied to those of women and other gender identities everywhere.

One day, while I am walking along the boulevard, a girl runs past, a few metres away from me, and knocks a mullah's turban into the air. Turban tipping started becoming popular two or three weeks into the protests. Every time I see a mullah, I now expect such a scene, but each time it happens in front of my eyes, I am still surprised.

I have not walked more than a few steps behind the mullah when the girl passes by like a flash of lightning. She throws the turban into the air with a fast chop of her hand, as though she has long awaited the moment with frustration and delight. She runs faster, getting farther and farther away, driven by happiness mixed with the horror of death, something one rarely sees in daily life. I hear the shouts of passers-by. Their applause makes the street tremble.

Any mullah who bends to pick up his turban at these moments comes face to face with an unwelcome realisation: when such audacity is possible, the situation is becoming alarming. And for the frightened mullah who heads the regime, there is only one path open: that of revenge.

Since we have been under the rule of the mullahs, this is the first time that people have ever chosen to directly insult them. And so, despite many not taking Iran's protests seriously, we ourselves know how far we have come.

Today, you see scenes reminiscent of the dream sequences in experimental films: mullahs who wrap their turbans around their chins with pieces of fabric; mullahs who do not wear their turbans any more. Seeing them alongside women who do not wear their headscarves any more, having renounced the hijab mandated by those very mullahs, we are transported to a surreal version of our homeland. We can see a pavement full of both afraid heads and unafraid heads.

It is during these days that a Muslim scholar from the city of Qom announces that Hazrat-e Mahdi's[7] turban was flipped as he was strolling incognito around the city, and that he is very upset with us all. Following that, videos go viral of mullahs' abayas, their outer robes, being removed as well as their turbans.

It is during one of my daily strolls that I happen upon a street event. It is the kind of moment in a country's historical memory that can become a great episode if it is allowed to do so. Or, if evil prevents this, it instead becomes an amnesiac void, which is what happens with most movements in the Middle East.

The protests get archived, simply marked with their beginning and ending dates. These moments are national acts of spiritual expression, even flashpoints for national miracles, but they can gradually be forgotten as a movement subsides. Pages from the history of Tunisia, Syria, Libya, Bahrain, Iraq, Egypt all get bundled together into the same container: that of the Arab Spring – and that's it. But what about the grand moments of these movements? Moments during which wounded protestors were cared for on the floors of shops in Aleppo. The first day that paintings appeared on the walls of schools in Daraa. The exact second when Bouazizi threw paint thinner over his head in front of the municipality building and started the flames of the Tunisian Revolution.

Or the moment I arrive at the sign for Hijab Street, right after it has been spray painted to read No-Hijab Street.

Above us, big white clouds are passing by quickly, and the drivers in the street have hit their brakes, pausing to read the sign. For us, this is the moment we know for sure that we are part of a major event.

When we enter the streets, we know that each and every one of us could at any moment end up like one of the protestors whose imprisonment and execution we hear of every day. The truth is, we head out to the streets with a rage that is both terrible and romantic. And that is our Achilles' heel. Our rage is so much greater than our logic, and sometimes it even made us believe that we could overthrow the regime without a leader or any kind of strategic plan.

From time to time, new information seeps out. Prisoners are transferred to hospitals and reports of rape and the rupture of sexual organs emerge, only for the victims to be returned to prison with minimum medical care, leaving hospital staff horrified.

When rumours spread, the regime responds by keeping protestors in prison until any traces of sexual assault have disappeared. If you ask me, these rumours are among the first successful blows to the movement. Hasn't our civil disobedience faced such responses in the past 40 years? Yes, it has. Is it outside of the regime's regular mechanisms of punishment? Not at all. So, how can such news create tiny cracks in our unity, causing bubbles of spreading horror?

Because we are just beginning to realise that our anger and hatred of the Islamic Republic are not enough to destroy it. They threaten it, make it insecure, frustrate it, make it more bloodthirsty – but they do not destroy it.

And yet, we keep going. We hope that our immense anger, as if omniscient, can cancel out the regime's blackmail. We rely on our anger and don't realise that it isn't a big enough resource.

Survival Iranian-style means moving the most alive parts of ourselves into the shadows.

We are a people for whom any form of nightlife in the past 44 years has constituted a crime punishable with everything from fines to lashing, and so we organise these nights of protest with extraordinary moral responsibility.

To outsiders, the nocturnal restrictions might seem delirious, an absurdity, the conditions of a deranged society. We have faced fines for our all-nighters; detainment for participating in any celebration not segregating women and men; lashes for drinking alcohol even when it's consumed in our own houses, sitting at the kitchen table, a glass in hand, crying from loneliness.

These are just some of the reasons why, in Iran, we have moved our nightlife underground. And still, during the Woman, Life, Freedom protests, we not only continue attending all kinds of parties and continue crying with a drink in our hand, sitting alone at our kitchen tables, but we have also begun shouting slogans at the top of our lungs every night at nine o'clock, in every neighbourhood of our cities.

Alone, behind our windowpanes, or together after stopping the music, our nightly ritual starts. Crying all the cries we cannot shout in the streets during the day: 'Woman / Life / Freedom!' 'Islamic Revolution / We don't want it / We don't want it!' 'Hey, hey / You sitting there motionless / The next Mahsa is one of you!' Like a wounded tribe, we call out for a miracle: 'Freedom / Freedom / Freedom!' And always, interspersed between all of these, you can hear another slogan: 'Death to Khamenei.'

This last one is not the outcome of just one or two years. For 1,400 years, we have called out at night – sometimes in our hearts, sometimes through writing on posters and flyers, and sometimes shouting from our rooftops – for the death of rulers whose systems we have been forced to serve during the day.

Where is the border between defiance and violence? After the third or fourth night, I stop shouting this last slogan. I simply stand there in darkness and listen. I do not want death. I do not want it.

I do not demand death, even for the interrogator who sat in front of me last year and built up a case against me – the interrogator whose shoes were so excessively polished, they pushed me to the verge of breakdown as I wondered for whose attention he could possibly have shined them. There is a part of me that thinks death is too romantic, that wants these men, from the top position all the way to the bottom, to be forced instead to take responsibility, to admit their complicity.

The frequency of our cries is different each night, depending on what news we heard that day: news of kids being shot at and killed; armed attacks on dorms and schools; regime forces surrounding a hospital that protestors have been admitted to.

We have for years been turning this life into an underground one. But, at its most brilliant, the nightlife of each city is a form of social ecstasy, one which is bound up with our fear of the patriarchal authorities. Our nocturnal gatherings are more incandescent than ever since the regime forces began marking the doors of houses where slogans can be heard. These marks mean that, in the morning, members of a house must await the knock of the law at their door.

During the night, we shout slogans behind the windows. During the day, all day, we are in the streets. But I still constantly feel I have missed something. Every morning, I wake up with a sense of paralysis. I immediately pick up my phone, and if the internet has been shut down, I feel like I am at the bottom of a well, as if the lid of a coffin has closed over me. I panic that I have been left behind. But if I am lucky and the internet is connected – even at a low speed – and the VPN I used last night is not yet blocked, then I rejoin the world of the living.

News of arrests, rapes, shootings and the corresponding resistance and mythical resolve of our people is the only news that can animate me. Mothers and fathers who sit outside prison doors and pace up and down all night. Activists who embroider *Woman, Life, Freedom* on fabric and are arrested, only to continue to embroider *Woman, Life, Freedom* in jail. The political prisoner who sews his lips together in protest. The woman who, right after being freed, stands in front of the prison doors and shouts slogans against Khamenei, only to be arrested again and sent back into the prison.

These people are connected to the myths of our national literature by invisible threads. Not to the stories themselves but to their spirit, their sense of being original, far-fetched, unearthly. Maybe hundreds of years from now, one of the well-known naqqals, the storytellers of our land, will go from city to city, publicly reciting these fables of our time, accompanying them with pictures from our streets instead of paintings from the *Book of Kings*.

They will hang these images on the wall and recite for their audience how, in the year 1401 of the Persian calendar, there was a young man who was killed at his steering wheel for the mere crime of honking during a street protest; that there was a girl who stood tall and strong by the gravestone of her mother, cutting her hair in protest; that there were mothers who danced at the graves of their kids, and fathers who held their children's long-wished-for wedding ceremonies in cemeteries, by the freshly dug, wet, cold earth; that there were lovers who slept all night long on the graves of their beloveds.

These are some of the most mythical, otherworldly events of the Woman, Life, Freedom movement. It is a mistake to think that they simply reflect the revolutionary aspects of this time. No. All these events also spring from the Persian language, from its literature and legacy: from scenes where heroes go deep into the sea, only to rise more alive than any prophets; from lines of poetry where protagonists must travel through the snowy land of death in order to kill monstrous divs; from the most celebrated story of all, in which the Iranians finally lock up Zahhak, a king who carries snakes on his shoulders, serpents that devour the minds of their land's youth.

Today's events reflect the glory of a language that has succeeded in expressing the darkest reaches of love, where

it nears pure madness. A language with subtleties that are
hard to translate into any other:

> *She embraced him tighter than she would her own soul.*
> *Having found her beloved, she forgot her own soul.*

> *The two bodies merged into one another as such*
> *That the soul of one became the shroud of the other.*[8]

You must be a Persian-language speaker to truly see how,
by the end of the last line, death runs through our arteries
alongside gentleness and love – an intravenous intoxicant.
In Persian, we do not read poetry; we consume it like
a drug.

Tahereh

After the attempted assassination of the King, Naser-eddin Shah, all the disciples of Babism were sentenced to death. The Babis were numerous enough for the King to make of them an extensive display of the variety of true Islam's punishments. Shiism in its most uncompromising form overtook the throne of judgement.

Students of theology skinned Babists using scissors and did so with exceptional skill. Their heads were suspended by ropes from city poles. Holes were made in the bodies of living captives, into which candles were planted – a job more delicate than that of the King's gardener in the royal greenhouse. Maybe one day I will write a story about the person tasked with lighting those candles.

A band of musicians was summoned to accompany the procession of those luminous, screaming bodies from the King's citadel to the city square. In the streets and bazaars, people showered them with insults, threw stones at them and learned the lessons they needed to learn.[9]

Why, then, did the King did not allow a finger to be laid on Tahereh? He said, 'I love her greatness. Let her live.'

And for three years, she was locked up on the top floor of the chief of police's house.

Like the scent of royal game roasting, news of her captivity spread beyond the borders of the city. What choice did the anxious Shiite courtiers have other than to bring forward the day of the woman's execution?

The most telling piece of gossip was that the King was smitten by Tahereh's intelligence and beauty. History tells us that the King asked for Tahereh's hand in marriage, but she refused. She found it more comfortable to live on the top floor of the chief of police's house than in the King's harem; but why so when there were already 2,000 other women living in the harem, 112 of them as the King's legitimate wives? She turned him down in a poem full of mockery and sarcasm:

> To you, the kingdom and splendour of Alexander.
> To me, the traditions and customs of Qalandars.
>
> If that is good, you enjoy it.
> If this is bad, I deserve it.[10]

It was a response similar to the one she gave her ex-husband, Mullah Mohammad, a few years earlier, after he sent a message asking her to reconcile. Her response to him, though, was in prose:

> Tell the stupid fool for me that … if you really loved me, you would come to meet me while I was in Karbala and you would walk with me on my journey from Karbala to Iran, putting yourself all the while at service.

Could Mullah Mohammad imagine himself carrying Tahereh's palanquin over his shoulders?

The following lines of the message were even sharper. Now that Mullah Mohammad had not carried out that service and three years had passed since their separation, Tahereh refused to allow a meeting between the two of them, neither in this world nor the next. She declared, 'I have renounced you, and you will not receive any further attention from me.'

A modern Western man might find Tahereh's responses provocative. For a man of that time, raised under Shiite chauvinism, they were boasts that could not be left without retaliation. After all, throughout history and around the world, patriarchy has depicted the attainment of women's rights as a perversity worthy of punishment.

Tahereh was not considered a first-rate poet, and Naser-eddin Shah was thought by many to have lost his wits, but even the addled King could interpret her message. Tahereh was well aware of the possible consequences of rejecting the most powerful man in the kingdom. She was revolting against the stupidity of the patriarchal system.

One is reminded here of Olympe de Gouges, the French-woman who, the previous century, said that if women could be sent to the guillotine, they could also speak at a podium. She was eventually sent to the guillotine.

Like Tahereh, we, too, are not unaware of the fate that awaits us. And often, when I walk the boulevard, I wonder what the people of her era thought about their own ending. Did they fear the King? Or ever imagine he would order them to be killed, as he had the Babists?

This boulevard I walk along now was once upon a time a miserable abandoned area on the fringes of the old city. Just a few streets away, 170 years ago, Tehran came to an end. Back then, the surrounding area was still a barren land – a dry desert, filled with thieves, muleteers, prostitutes, gypsies and people with various diseases.

In the mornings, jugglers and their dressed monkeys smoked opium together and passed through the city gates high and happy, looking for a corner to put on a performance, hoping people would throw them some money. In the evening, strongmen called pahlevans,[11] who had spent the day putting on shows in which they tore apart thick chains, returned home tired, yearning after a woman or a man who had thrown them a coin or two earlier. The naqqals went to cafés and city squares and, with the help of painted canvases, recited stories from the *Book of Kings* or ancient Persian myths.

No, 170 years ago, neither the naqqal who went to sleep over his painted canvas, nor the geomancer who swirled his brass cubes before throwing them – all the while melting a lump of opium in the tea he prepared over a wood fire – needed to fear that they might end up killed by the State, like Tahereh and the Babists.

The night that Tahereh was murdered, the gypsies gathered around their fires with their musical instruments, pots and pans, and opium pipes. They were busy laughing, making love and having fights. The next night, when the news reached them, they might have even made jokes. The same was true of the residents on the other side of the city borders, the ones considered a bit more civilised.

Eventually, following the horrific punishments ordered by the King, terror did what it always does, and fewer and fewer people talked about Babism or about the famous Tahereh.

One day, as I walk over the remains of the old bounds of the city, I suddenly come upon a poignant, familiar scene. Three high-school girls, wearing navy-blue uniforms, have pulled down their maghna'ehs[12] all the way to their shoulders.

They wear the same mandatory, military-like uniforms that I, too, was forced into for years when in school. Joseph Brodsky once said that schools in the Communist Soviet Union were both prisons and factories.[13] I want to add that schools are barracks, too. But the students I see here in the street are a sharp contrast to the soldiers around them. The girls' purposeful walk is an act of resistance in the face of military oppression; it is a refusal to submit, a rejection of State power.

They are women disregarding their uniforms, standing against men whose very identity comes from their uniforms.

At first, there are only three girls. Then another one runs over from the other side of the boulevard and joins them – then two more, as they arrive at the overpass. Their individual steps cannot be heard, but their march sounds like the march of many. I start to follow them. The glowing, subdued light of the evening shines on them; sometimes a fiery sunbeam catches their chestnut hair.

30

The protestors' hair is not the hair you see in Persian miniatures. Its twists and turns are not decorative, unlike the hair of the women drawn by male miniaturists from one school of painting or another over hundreds of years.[14]

The illustrated women appear in the midst of a frenzy of colours that sometimes reaches pure chaos. Women dancing, playing instruments, reading letters. Women who always look passive, completely in the service of what is expected of them. Women who are irresistible, even seductive – not for the men inside the miniatures, but for those watching them from outside the frame. These women were always drawn for a male audience.

As such, the male painters, perhaps instinctively, subjected the women of Persian miniatures to the same treatment they gave the landscapes, cities and buildings they depicted: they lack depth.[15]

The aesthetic standards of these miniatures originated in literature. The curls and twists of hair are reminders of Persian calligraphy. Round breasts are inspired by poetry, which compares them to pomegranates. Downy hair appears above lips; this was said to mean that only adolescent boys and women could be perfect lovers.

Within these miniatures, women who were in reality confined to the house and forced to live sequestered in interior wings were depicted sitting freely by rivers or in plains. While real women were trapped indoors, the waves of the illustrated women's jet-black hair were meant to remind the viewer of stormy seas or hunting grounds full of secret traps supposed to capture each and every passer-by, leading them to their death. In literature, women's hair was even compared to slaughterhouses full of decapitated heads.

Such descriptions were in alignment with an Islamic belief in the sinfulness of women's hair and the necessity of its conceal-ment. The more violently a woman's body tempted desire, the more legitimate were the patriarchal rules that ordered it covered.

And thus, the necessity of maintaining authority over female bodies became a matter of fact, with no room for conver-sation or negotiation. While barely dressed women found their way into Persian miniatures, women in real, everyday life wore clothing even more modest than men's: trousers down to their ankles and long tunics.

Throughout history, who would have imagined that the aesthetics of female hair would be transformed from the sentimental and sensuous representations found in art into what we see today? Letting our hair loose is a protest against patriarchal rules, a manifestation of our right to our own bodies, a right demanded and fought for, in one way or another, all around the world in the present century. The hair of the high-school girls and all the women in the streets of Iran today is combat attire.

All of us who walk along the pavement see from a distance the security guards standing in front of their motorcycles at the upcoming crossroads. The street suddenly grows a few decibels quieter; I am certain it is not my mind playing tricks on me.

And then the yelling starts: 'Wear your hijabs.' It is one of the motorcyclists, who is coming closer to the girls. But they ignore him, continuing to chat loudly about their day, about the events of that other military base: the school. The cars and pedestrians all slow down, and once again, there is yelling: 'Wear your hijabs.' This time, the girls grow silent. But none of them stop walking; none of them even touches their maghna'ehs. Another guard, who is listening to his walkie-talkie – perhaps to an order – walks to the first guard and tells him something, and then he steps back and grows silent.

For a second, I think that we, too, like our city, could perhaps survive.

The history of hijab in Iran is a complex one; women's right to choose their clothing has been subject to the wishes of the rulers throughout its modern history.

In 1936, Reza Shah, the first King of the Pahlavi dynasty, saw the removal of the hijab as one of the key symbols of Western development and modernity. First, he brought his own wife and two daughters into the streets without a hijab or face covering. Then, with the same determination, he began building railways and bridges.

He decided to make the city respectable. Policemen's batons came down on the skulls of citizens who urinated in the streets. Nobody knows how many slaps and kicks were delivered before people stopped sacrificing camels. This ritual had been carried out during religious festivities; camels with slit throats roamed the streets while Muslims ran after them with knives.

The removal of hijabs was now mandated and enforceable by violence. Policemen pulled veils from women's heads while beating them,[16] in the same streets where, 43 years later, the Islamic Republic would use batons on women's bodies to make wearing the hijab mandatory.[17] Before the 1979

Revolution, not wearing the Islamic dress code was considered a sign of right-thinking modernity; after the Revolution, it became a sign of vice and moral corruption.

And the story continues today, when traditional sticks have been replaced by modern imported batons. We are fighting so that the men in power do not continue to measure the extent of their empire's virtue by their ability to decide how women clothe their bodies.

Between the months of Aban (October–November) and Dey (December–January), in late 2022 and early 2023, horrible news about the movement and Tehran's pollution compete with one another. The Islamic Republic burns more and more mazut-heavy fuel oil in its power plants, making the weather outside our windows darker and more toxic. Then, we receive the news of a student falling into a coma. She was beaten in the head with a baton for having set fire to photographs of Khomeini and Khamenei.

Every morning, I sit on the living-room carpet, with a cup of tea in hand, worried and scared, searching for any news of her. She looks like the schoolgirls I saw in the streets. I'm hoping for her to wake up. She is a 16-year-old who, the Islamic Republic claims, obtained her injuries when she attempted to commit suicide by throwing herself out of her school bus because she was dealing with mental health issues. Many other teenagers of her age, if they remain alive after arrest, are being sent to correctional facilities under similar cover stories of alleged mental instability.

Sitting in the grey light, with my tea turning cold, I read about doctors losing hope of the girl waking up. I see her awakening as a symbol of our hope. I imagine that if she comes back to our world, it will be an auspicious omen for us.

All this relates back to what I witnessed that day on the boulevard with the high-school girls. The hope for this girl's survival is the sole spear with which I defend myself against the events of that day.

And finally, after a few months, she comes back to us. She regains consciousness. And since that day, no matter where I go, I take within my dark body a small, warm flame of hope.

One afternoon, I find myself in the streets slightly to the south of the boulevard. I didn't deliberately head there, but I have to escape in that direction. The regime has begun to shoot at protestors' eyes, targeting one or both. It's their newest method for identifying the protestors as soon as they arrive at hospitals. When pellets are targeted at the arms, the legs or the back, you can usually find a way to pull them out, bandage the wound and survive. But with a pellet in the eye, you have to go to hospital, knowing all too well that you could lose part of your eyesight. And the hospitals won't perform the extraction unless you sign a forced confession statement.

The boulevard is getting darker and the number of the guards greater. White light from shops brightens the pavement, but the large LED lamps illuminate only their immediate surroundings. On the walls, the anti-regime graffiti slogans are crossed out or covered up, which makes me curious. I come to myself and realise that I am standing in front of a wall, trying to decipher the words; a line, a point, a phrase sometimes reveals itself. The very redactions become an attraction, inviting me to imagine all types of slogans and insults.

With our overfull minds, we cannot do much more than walk. We must stay in the streets and tire out the regime's forces. As we do, their gangs of motorcycles suddenly drive onto the pavements, quickly, in file, honking, forcing us to step out of their way. They carry this out with exceptional control and order. If I am lucky, their batons strike the air and do not land on me. If I am unlucky, they leave traces that can last on my body for a month.

This evening, out in the street, I suddenly sense that a man has been following me, only a few steps behind, for two blocks. He must have realised that I have noticed him. He steps closer and whispers something behind me: 'Agents of the regime outnumber the people.'

I have heard a lot about plain-clothes guards approaching people in cafés and streets to gather information about protests. Rumours say that they talk about the riot police's weapons in order to frighten people off.

The man repeats once again: 'The remorseless outnumber the people.' Does he hope that I will respond? What does he expect? Is he just a lonely man? Is he psychotic or wanting to scare people? Or is he one of the murderers who have found unique new opportunities in the turbulent city? Nothing can be excluded. I don't know. If he was one of us, why would he say these words? Why repeat them over and over? Why is he pointing out what I can see for myself? The first rule these days is not to speak to anyone. And if anyone speaks to you, consider them either mad, a murderer or a regime officer.

I can see from a distance that the end of the boulevard is emptying out. Anxiety spreads from my neck to my earlobes, my heart pounding. The plain-clothes guards are too many among us. They do not even feel the need to hide themselves. Every few metres, you see them standing on the sides, watching the people.

But there is something different about this guy. I do not exactly know what he is capable of. I am scared of him. The next time he repeats that regime agents outnumber the people, I turn around and look at him directly. He wears a cap, a mask and clothes just like thousands of other people in the city.

When we see these agents, what happens to our fear? Where does it go? How is it that rage takes over? I just stand there in the street and stare him in the eyes. He walks by me and immediately crosses the road. I see him walking down the boulevard, back in the same direction he was coming from – perhaps looking for another person to accost.

When I reach the end of the boulevard, I turn south. I do not pass anyone until I cross one of the squares south of the city. In one corner, around 15 women and men gather around a bonfire, burning scarves, as is our habit these days. It is impossible for a fire to be set up in a neighbourhood without women – often dancing and whirling – throwing their scarves into it. Even when protestors set rubbish bins on fire just to close off the streets and protect against guards, I always see women running towards the fire and throwing their rolled-up maghna'ehs or scarves into the flames. Hijabs are like the petrol in our Molotov cocktails: fuel for the revolution.

This is one of the grand moments I'm talking about – moments that seem to mark the beginning of national miracles. Even though I have come face to face with such events dozens of times, I still feel, every time I arrive at them, that we are sitting on the shoulders of giants, surveying the territories we have conquered.

It has been a long while now since I stopped wearing a hijab, so I never have a scarf with me to set on fire, but every time I happen on a moment like this, I feel all our thousand-years-old wars have been nothing but a long prelude to a book containing only this one sentence: women will take back agency over their bodies.

On this evening, in this particular neighbourhood, all these complexities are, however, tainted with a sense of sorrow I do not even try to push away after a few minutes. I know that no writer has ever been able to build a mausoleum out of literature, a place where the dead can find peace. Literature, after all, aims to stir up the lives of both the living and the dead. Even when a writer writes a eulogy, they must still bring the dead back from their eternal peace to this world.

I want to do so now, to speak of the people whose horrifying murders might be familiar to Iranians but are not familiar to the world. People who in 1979 lived in this neighbourhood and who, one night, were surrounded by a zealous crowd of revolutionaries and fanatic Hezbollahi Muslims. Women who died by fire in just a few hours – right in front of the eyes of the firefighters who, according to later reports, had been ordered not to put the fire out. These women were called 'residents of the neighbourhood of sorrow', even though the neighbourhood's official name was 'Shahr-e No' ('The New City').

After the Pahlavi monarchy, the last monarchy in Iran, came to power in 1925, its rulers destroyed the harems of the Qajars, the preceding dynasty. They expelled the women

42

of the harem to the fringes of the city. The women were sent to this neighbourhood, as if they were mere objects whose lustre and usefulness to the royal household had expired. Many of the women had never stepped outside the courtyard of the palace's women's wing. The only landscape most of them had seen was the hunting grounds they had looked at through their veils while accompanied by the King. How many of them could realistically turn to sewing, hairdressing or playing music to make a living?

It didn't take long for the neighbourhood to be transformed into a red-light district, policed according to regulatory controls that the ruling men devised for the women's bodies. And from then on, until the 1979 Islamic Revolution, the neighbourhood housed an amalgamation of brothels, bars and cabarets.

The significance of these women and their pimps should not be disregarded. Some of them were believed to work in the service of the King's court. At some political junctures, they invaded the oppositions' houses, along with city thugs, or spoke on the radio in favour of the King, playing the role of random citizens.

The women had dreams: dreams of paying back their debts to their pimps and leaving the neighbourhood behind, even though they knew too well that would be impossible; dreams of even opening their own brothels. In 1979, all these dreams, along with the money saved inside pillows and mattresses to help to realise them, went up in flames.

What happens to the dreams of a person who has longed over and over again to escape a room and, in the end, is burned to death one night in that same room?

Every time I hear the news of the killing or execution of a protestor, I once again ask myself this question: what about that person's dreams? The moments in their life when they envied something, wished for more. The tears, the regrets, the yearnings. What happens to them? Where do they go? Since September 2022, for the first time ever, we have been screaming these questions in the face of history.

What propelled the revolutionary forces of Iran's 1979 Revolution was the same phenomenon Montaigne names as the spark behind the religious wars of 16th century France: the victory of passion over wisdom. This is the Christian model. When it comes to the Islamic model and the revolutionary fanatic Muslims of the 1979 Revolution, one should add unbridled religious dogmatism to the mix. This, like the wrong dose of drugs at a party, threw the country into pandemonium.

A regime that got its totalitarian legitimacy from its religion, was, before anything else, in need of a villainous cleverness, an ingenuity that would allow it to devise all kinds of methods to get rid of its opponents and prisoners, calling them apostate, renegade and corrupt.

In the fiery massacre of Shahr-e No, first the pimps were arrested and pulled out, only to be executed later one after another. Who decided to separate them before setting all the others on fire? Were the others burned because they were sinful according to the Islamic law of Sharia? Were they being paid back for having historically sided with the ousted King? Or had they seen and known things that they were not supposed to see and know?

Between blinding prostitutes with smoke before burning them alive and shooting the current protestors in the eyes, isn't the message one and the same? The cost of being a witness.

Tahereh

To write is to testify; to exhume, to dig deep wells.

The well into which Tahereh was thrown is only a few roads south of the boulevard where I walk with the others. When she did not stop exposing the injustices of her time, when she refused to submit to the King's marriage proposal, she was convicted of murder. A crime was invented to justify her execution.

No court session was held, and she did not defend herself in any hearing. And yet, it seems hard to believe that, when they came for her in the middle of the night, to take her from the chief of police's house to the Ilkhani garden, she did not know where she was going.

Just like the protestors who have received execution sentences in the past few months.

They were all executed early in the morning, right at the moment of the call to prayer. Almost all of them had spoken to their lawyers the previous day and were waiting their release from prison; they were hopeful.

In the mornings, I often wake to the news of one or another protestor having been executed a few hours earlier. Then my body once again becomes paralysed, while my mind does not stop. Putting all its masochistic forces to work, it drives me to the limits of obsession and despair. I retrace each and every second of that morning's execution, as if it is my own memory.

They come for you during the night, wake you up, take you to a separate cell. This part of the prison is known for its strong winds and for its solitary-confinement cells, used for prisoners on execution watch. You do not believe it. You tell yourself they are just trying to scare you. At the time of the call to prayer, they open the door to the cell. You tell them they have no right to do this. They drag you through the cold prison courtyard under swirling snowflakes that smell of metal. Without informing your parents or your lawyer, they carry out a sentence decreed only a few hours earlier, without you even being present.

We are a nation not unfamiliar with savagery. It is as old
as our history, and it is with this injury that we keep running
through the streets, sometimes even dying.

Seeing the schoolgirls marching reminds me of another
unforgettable episode from our history. Our modern school
system is not that old – it has been around for less than 200
years. The first few schools received a totally predictable
reception: they were blown up with gunpowder, disappearing into thin air. According to the fatwas of the clerics,
schools were the weapons of devil armies, come to combat
religious teachings. Many worried they were Christianity's
way of covertly attacking Islam. And what need did we
have for modern schools when there were traditional maktab
classes in every neighbourhood?

These classes held in mosques or in the houses of neighbourhood mullahs had survived for centuries. Their key
function was to keep the kids out of the house for a few
hours every day. There was no need to teach them anything
other than the Quran, the Persian alphabet and some maths.
The good thing about these classes was that, for the smallest
violation, you could hit the kids with a stick on the sole of
their feet. That was considered a necessary spur for their

personal growth. In exchange for these services, the parents paid the maktab mullah with food or money.

The introduction of modern schools was going to diminish the mullah's control over the public and bring one of their sources of income to a stop. The schools were going to teach innocent kids not only the Quran, the alphabet, addition and subtraction, but also pernicious sciences that would undermine God. They would defame the maktabs by allowing rumours of mullahs' paedophilia to spread.

Girls' schools were the ultimate affront. One of the most influential clerics of the time called them brothels. One mosque's mullah threatened that, if women's rights activists didn't stop such debauchery and prostitution (meaning the founding of girls' schools), he would mobilise crowds to attack the schools and destroy them, drowning them in spit. Inevitably, the hand of God had to come out of his devout believers' sleeves and cleanse the land of these new institutions, with the use of explosives.

Any testimony turns the life of the witness providing it upside down, even before it is a thorn in the side of the accused. I was only a year old when I gave my first testimony. It was during a time when Tehran was trembling under Iraqi missile attacks, and the first words I uttered, after 'Father' and 'Mum', were nothing other than, 'Turn it off.'

When the sirens announced an incoming attack, my parents took me, wrapped in a blanket, in their arms, and we ran down the stairs into the basement. Amid the sound of the deafening alarm and our scared, unsure steps on the staircase, one of the neighbours shouted at someone who had a cigarette or a flashlight on, 'Turn it off! Turn it off!' They thought that the smallest source of light could make us easy targets for the Iraqi planes.

We found refuge in the basement, where the darkness saved us. In my one-year-old mind, 'Turn it off!' was as much associated with security as the words 'Mum' and 'Father'. 'Turn it off' was my first testament to the land I had been born into.

That war went on for eight years, and all the while other bloody projects were also under way. Fanatical faith found its

51

satisfaction in perpetuating violence: mass executions; nightly arrests; the assassination of the previous regime's supporters, along with confiscation of their property; the implementation of the mandatory hijab; and the Cultural Revolution.

Anyone who had not fully assimilated into the new regime eventually received news of the arrest or killing of an old friend or close family member. Most nights, there was a blackout. My parents talked with their friends at the kitchen table, gathered around candle flames or lamps powered by oil bought with ration coupons. They talked about friends or family members executed in prison. About a friend whose baby was born in prison and had to grow up in there with their mother. A few months or years later, yet other problems would arise. How would they tell the kid that their father had been executed? And who would deliver the news to them that their mother, too, was scheduled for execution?

We have a hard time comprehending why my generation's parents – the mothers and fathers who wrapped us in blankets, held us under their arms and ran down the stairs to the basements – have been conservatively passive in the face of the regime for the last 44 years.

The foundations of their parenting always rested on fear and dissembling. We were told not to speak at school about having alcohol at home. We were not supposed to even tell our friends that, at parties held at our house, the family men and women danced side by side. We were not to tell others that our fathers cursed Khomeini over dinner.

Our parents did not realise how this system of raising us, with the pretext of protecting us, little by little turned our homes into extensions of the dictatorship. Even the ones who were most opposed to the regime's principals forced us to simply say 'yes' to the religious and political aspects of our schooling: 'Just say yes and obey the rules. Let this school year pass so you can graduate to the next level.'

But they were also the ones who taught us how to survive our loneliness in a world where we could not trust in or rely on others.

If, with a perfectionism beyond logic, they wanted us to be the best in everything we did, it was because they thought that, then, the regime would not be able to harm us as easily. And perhaps our achievements would even allow us to leave our country one day and live elsewhere.

For our parents' generation, that was how resistance was defined: we were their only means of resistance, their secret path to survival. In an era of suffocation and mass murders, they saw resistance in living discreet underground lives in smart ways. A subterranean life beneath the nose (and beard) of the Islamic Republic was the only way to avenge the compromises they had made with the regime. And their only way to appease their consciences.

But our parents, like tree-trunks, were made of concentric layers, coating after coating of fear for their survival. And once the fear settled deep in their bodies, they were never able to change, to make different kinds of choices.

The generation that had survived revolution, executions and war believed they had survived because they were clever – or because they were lucky. They never imagined that they were alive because, in the eyes of the regime, their time had not yet come. Or that, when it did, all their discretion would become meaningless.

This attitude has been the difference between my parents' generation and those following them since the beginning of the 2022 uprising. And perhaps it's the main reason behind the generational differences between protestors. Why is the biggest wave of protest against a 44-year-old regime composed of university students, high-schoolers and teenagers? These young people have lived only for a decade to a maximum of 25 years under the Islamic Republic. Is it the enthusiasm of youth? Yes, surely, but these kids also make up a generation raised in more humane and fair communities, where their right to choose and their right to self-determination were not considered anathema to survival.

No one asked this generation to adopt total obedience and secrecy. They did not have parents like our parents; theirs were people who, at their age, had done all they could to free themselves from the yoke of endless acquiescence and domestic totalitarianism. When my generation walk alongside their kids in the protests, when they rejoice for the martyrdom of their kids, they are revolting against all the 'yes'es they were forced to utter in the face of both domestic and political patriarchy.

Because of the presence of the oppressive older generation, in the first days following the killing of Mahsa-Jina Amini, no one knew how far things would go. Like previous protests, we started by merely gathering in the streets. We were desperate witnesses testifying to a murder. We could turn a blind eye to it, the way our parents had done to previous crimes, or instead we could directly denounce it. And that's exactly what we did.

Despite the historical caveats circling us like tormented ghosts, we could feel a collective event rushing towards us in full force, inciting us to leave our homes. We knew that if we didn't come out, tomorrow it would be our turn to be arrested, killed, executed or barred from our jobs and classes. The murder of Mahsa-Jina opened our eyes, uniting us in understanding a collective tragedy. She left our world and passed on to another, ushering us, too, into a new age.

In going against our survival mechanisms and inherited cautiousness, the response to the killing of Mahsa-Jina was the starting point of our biggest psychological revolution – a revolution to the depth of our genes.

When a week went by and the streets did not clear out, we knew that, this time, it was different.

There is no way that we are going back to how we lived before. We are afraid, but we have moved beyond our fears and stepped out into the streets. We hover on the high of our terror, the same way our mystics moved above the dark waters of the ocean of calamities and catastrophes.[18]

Under the influence of our new-found unity, everything has been transformed – right down to its foundation. Our view of history has become crystal clear. Our criticism of the past is unprecedented. Our position towards family, religion and patriarchy is blunt and bold.

From this point on, we know that, regardless of whether our political system changes or not, we have rerouted its trajectory forever.

There are particular moments that make new people join the movement or that strengthen the engagement of those who are already part of it. Moments when women stand without their hijabs in a line in front of a wall of policemen; when civil rights activists send messages from inside the prisons where they are tortured; when lawyers who represent political activists are imprisoned themselves; when protestors are executed. If you listen carefully, within each of these moments, you can hear a judge's hammer sounding in a court session in which the whole country is put on trial. After each, both the regime and the people arrive, over and over again, at a shared conclusion: nothing will ever go back to how it was before the killing of Mahsa-Jina Amini.

Female athletes take off their hijabs in international competitions, only to be arrested upon their arrival back in the country and forced into public fake confessions. On social media, theatre groups share videos of anti-regime performances. We throw buckets of paint over officially sanctioned street murals, mostly images of military men. We hang posters from pedestrian bridges, bearing the names of loved ones murdered by the regime. We turn the water in the public ponds and fountains blood red. We want everyone to wake up and see what is happening. It is as if we are trying to send telegraphic messages to the earth's inhabitants from another planet.

We compose Persian songs using old revolutionary chants from other nations. We are not lacking in new ones either. But the main hymn of our movement, the one that takes over the world, is not an epic anthem. Its lyrics are not even written by one person. Every line comes from an unknown individual in a corner of our land, all of them pointing to our old, shared and familiar regrets, underlining why we have joined together to embody this collective tragedy. The 'Baraye' ('For') song is a collective eulogy protesting years of suffocation and rejection.[19] It is the song of a nation whose citizens have been deprived of the primary rights that are considered normal for other people, rights that should be an unexceptional part of everyday life.

TV and film stars are not as luminous as before. Actresses – even those who participated for years in regime-sponsored projects – publish photographs of themselves without the hijab. Celebrities are learning lessons from the public out in the streets. Everyone wants to rub shoulders with the nameless women and men who march, suddenly transformed into great gods. Everyone is reading books about either dictators or women's rights: the patriarchs and the feminists wage war in the front lines of bookshop windows. From translations of *The School for Dictators* to *How to be a Dictator*, from 'Is Our Name Remembered?' to *We Should All Be Feminists*.[20] From the lives of dictators who have come and gone to the lives of feminists who have left their trace on the patriarchal body forever.

But I cannot read anything other than poetry these days – mainly Pessoa. I wander through his words the same way I wander around the back streets of Tehran. As I pass nearby college students who stamp their feet and shout slogans, I have an immense longing to see what Pessoa once saw.

As I turn a corner in our tumultuous city, I imagine finding myself in the streets that, in his whispering poems, are sites for pausing, for stopping and catching one's breath. Like the aliases Pessoa created for himself, maybe I, too, am doubling: one version of me wanders real streets during the day and the other lingers in imaginary ones at night, looking for some peace.

Sometimes, I also turn to the poetry of Nosrat Rahmani, Iranian poet and opium lover. After his death in 2000, many prayers and spells were found in his house, talismans that were said to have been hidden by his wife so that she could keep him for herself. But when he spoke of streets and alleys in his poems, it was to write about following a mistress through them, after leaving the tavern dead drunk. In his poetry, he dreamed, and I stroll around in his dreams.

> *I dream.*
> *I dream I am free.*
> *I dream there are no chains around my feet.*
> *I dream I am a cloud raining over every house.*
> *I dream I am wind blowing through every tunnel.*

And then he seems to make a sudden turn:

> *I dream I am melancholic.*
> *I dream that, next to the wild Golpar bushes,*
> *I am washing someone's destiny with the tears of my eyes.*

Sometimes, though, I give in to temptation, reading about lives that have been lost to traumas of power. Usually at night – almost as if I am doing something behind my own back – I reach out and gently pick up a book by Anna Akhmatova. After all, she witnessed the most deranged regime of all time.

We are constantly receiving signs that reassure us this movement is different from all the previous ones. Beyond the
individual statements and complaints we write under our
own names, different professions regularly put out signed
petitions condemning the regime. Before this, rarely did
anyone, from labourers to doctors to teachers to lawyers,
dare to put their real name under statements full of condem-
nations of the Islamic Republic, for fear of the consequences.

We are known for being a forgetful nation, but every
writer and translator who signed the most recent open
letter against censorship – exclaiming that they will, from
now on, publish their work without censorship through
any possible channels – remembers all too well what
happened to those who signed the statement now known
as the 'Letter of the 134'. This open letter was signed and
published by 134 writers in 1994 with the title 'We Are
Writers'. It was protesting the censorship and constant
interrogations they had to put up with.

Following the letter, most of these writers were banned
from publishing their works for many years, and the permits
for their previous works were also revoked. Many of them
were taken to interrogation rooms. The destiny of two of

them became tied to the Chain Murders of Iran.[21] One of them was kidnapped when he was out grocery shopping, and the other when he was on his way to his bookshop. Mohammad Mokhtari's body was found by a road outside Tehran leading to a cement factory. Ahmad Mir Alai's body was found close to his house, with traces of two insulin injections on his arm. I wish their names, along with the names of many others killed, could be added to the open letter of Mahsa-Jina's movement.

Today, the regime implements creative new methods. They use online food and car apps to trace protestors and arrest them. They even present a few of those arrested as the killers of protestors – protestors, especially children, who were killed by the regime itself – in an attempt to wash their own hands of these murders.

Everyone is arrested. Everyone is convicted. This regime, which has done everything in its power for many years to kill off hope and humanity, is now becoming terrified, seeing that very hope and humanity revived in a completely different form. As such, it is left with no choice but to fall back on its old familiar techniques of assassination and intimidation, of manipulating testimony and corrupting the meaning of being a witness.

Tahereh

Tahereh has always been a seductive figure. Some consider her stubborn and hot-headed. Some find her total submission to Babism antithetical to her freedom-seeking. Others consider her connection to Babism to be one of blind devotion, rather than a deliberate opposition to Islam. If she had stayed alive, and if she had gained even a little bit of power (an impossible hypothesis), would she have changed the direction of Iranian culture to some degree?

Many years later, Iran's National Bank rose above the well into which Tahereh was thrown. The building was constructed by a German designer called Heinrich. A mixture of Iranian and European architecture made it a baroque edifice with column capitals in the shape of Achaemenid bulls. Eventually, it was transformed into the bank's museum, showcasing early banknotes and minting machines for the first Iranian coins.

Every time I pass it, I wonder how long decomposed bodies can survive within the memory of buildings. It is not the only one of this city's structures with a corpse at its foundation.

In December 2017, during excavations for Tehran's sewage system, the 7,000-year-old skeleton of a woman was found, pushing the age of the city way back into deep history. Traces of infection were found in her bones. Some said maybe she had been just a traveller passing through Tehran but not a city resident. Her skeleton was sent to Iran's National Museum so that the public could look at it.

In the autumn and winter of 2022, the bodies of several teenage girls were suddenly found by the foot of buildings around the city. The Islamic Republic announced that they had died falling off those buildings. In reality, officials had taken the girls' corpses to the tops of the buildings and thrown them down, only then calling the girls' families.

As a nation with many religious conflicts, we have come to accept that our history books are bloated by images of such murders, bloody conflicts and Shiite massacres. Our ideological punishments have hardly undergone a renaissance. Sticking metal forks into nostrils, donning clothes covered in gunpowder on people and setting them on fire in public squares ... Today, the methods of killing might have changed, but the motivations behind them have not.

Savagery has not only been part of our national way of life; it has also played an integral role in it. We have a book entitled *The History of Hard Killing*, which is an extensive compendium of various tortures, punishments and ways of killing opponents – often, those who opposed the idea of Shiite Islam and had faith, instead, in perpetual doubt.

Those who warn against Muslim patriarchy in Iran today must face this savagery.

For many centuries now, one of our greatest legends has been that of Rostam. He is one of the heroes of the *Book of Kings* and uses all kinds of magic and supernatural powers in a fight against his own son, Sohrab, eventually taking his life. Isn't it strange that, despite several stories in the book in which fathers and grandfathers are murdered, our most popular myth remains that of a filicide?

What did you expect? Filicide is the ultimate act of a patriarch. And in Iran, no father, especially if he is a hero of his people, loses a fight to his son.

It is said that Ferdowsi, the creator of the *Book of Kings*, refused to write his poems in Arabic. Was this rooted in language fanatism? Was it a sign of resistance against the invaders' language? Or, as it has been said, was it that, in his extraordinary wisdom, he realised that the best tool to write about and critique the nationality engraved in his DNA was Persian, the very language of that nation?

He achieved such mastery of the language – and thus of its people – that he succeeded in turning the hidden roots of our national ideology into characters, as if breathing a soul into the body of each and every one of our inherited beliefs.

His mythologies are harsh criticisms that, in his time, either could not exist or, if they did, could not be disseminated.

Like all writers who acquire the rank of prophet, Ferdowsi, too, went through transcendent suffering to create his characters. An example of his obsessive precision and subtlety can be seen in Rostam and Sohrab's filicide scene. The poet seems to say Rostam does not know that the beautiful man in front of him is his own son. But there are signs in the poem that hint at him knowing this all too well. Ferdowsi did not explicitly impose on Iranians the eternal sin of having knowingly killed their own children. But he did not hold back on implicitly criticising them either.

We have always preferred to think that Rostam did not recognise his son. Otherwise, we would have to lay our legends down on the autopsy table and, with the scalpel of realism, reveal their filicide. Maybe then, we would understand why, in our land, we can witness the murder of a child by their own parents, in all its indecency.

The Western Renaissance denounced child-killing with its progressive writings. But Islamic patriarchy, which is essentially incapable of renaissance – and which has, like Orthodox Judaism and Christianity, actually never claimed to be enlightened – has remained frozen in the moment of Abraham's decision to sacrifice his son Ismael.[22] The Islamic regime in Iran has given itself the right to shape the country's courts, its legal codes and its parliamentary laws and regulations, following the Islamic law word for word: a belief system in which paternal butchery is not a problem.

There is no difference between parents who cut their children into pieces and throw them in the bin and the dozens of fathers who every year kill their daughters for the question of honour. When it comes to filicide, on the basis of Islamic law: a) the father is the beneficiary and guardian of the child, and b) he cannot sue himself, so c) after a few years of imprisonment, he can be freed and go back to his family. The problem gets even simpler when we know that the legal guardian of a married woman is her husband.

Even with such a horrible prior image, the most horrifying aspect of the regime's response to the current uprising has been the killing of young kids.

One morning, I hear of the killing of an 8-year-old girl who left home to buy bread with her sister; they were both wearing their beautiful Baluchi clothes, their cheap plastic slippers. When she got shot with a bullet, she simply voiced one sentence: 'They shot me.' And then the 8-year-old died.

It is a real shame for fairy tales that none of these murdered kids return miraculously to the world of living. All the frogs and princes and speaking trees quickly turned their faces away when the 9-year-old boy who dreamed of becoming a robotic scientist – what happens to his dreams? – was killed. He was going back home with his parents and brother when their car was targeted by the bullets of Islamic Republic forces. The boy could not hide under the seat because he was, in his mother's words, a little chubby. The boy was shot at. The boy was killed.

He is survived by a mother who writes every day on her social media, asking questions about the shower of bullets that penetrated the body of her son and paralysed her husband. Eventually, she was fired from the school she taught at. The Islamic Republic has added one more woman to the army of mothers who have for years been oscillating between prison and the graves of their children, repeating the now-famous sentence: 'We will become your nightmare.'

These mothers have succeeded in doing this more than the regime ever expected – so much so that it has been forced to send baton-carrying messengers to give them a good lesson, which they do in quiet back streets or even by their children's gravestones.

The fathers of the children make graveside speeches that, without any need for literary devices, are the most poetic lamentations, simple but unbearably touching – speeches that are nothing less than court sessions, which put the Islamic Republic on trial and whose nobility elevates them far beyond legal statements. When, at the end of one such speech, a father states, 'I offer my child as a gift to Iran,' the sentence is an arrow fired from the bow of his grief, aimed at the eyes of the Islamic Republic.

These mothers and fathers are not the kind our patriarchal regime expects, because, in the furnaces of their grief, they have welded the steel of their mourning into weapons of resistance and struggle.

These parents who visit the graves of each other's children, these men who show up to work or walk in the streets wearing maghna'ehs to protest the humiliation women suffer due to their mandatory hijabs – these activists must surely drive the patriarchs to hopeless disbelief.

I have never met any of these mothers and fathers in person. But once, a woman who comes to clean our house tells me that the daughter of one of her neighbours has been shot in the streets and the regime is refusing to give her corpse back to the family.

This is not the first time the Islamic Republic has done this. There have even been times since 1979 when it has made families pay for the bullets used to kill their loved ones. They count the number of bullets found in a corpse and bill accordingly. Families have to pay in order to retrieve the body of their child, their brother, their sister, their father or their mother, and to be able to bury them.

I ask the woman how old the young woman was, whether she was a college student. She says no, says the young woman worked at a hair accessory shop, was killed when she went out to protest on one of the days that there were calls for strikes. Then she shows me pictures on her phone of the regime guards standing watch in front of the young woman's house.

She was shot six times; each bullet is priced at ten million tomans. Given the neighbourhood the woman is from, her family will not manage to save that much even over two years. All the neighbours join in helping to collect the money.

The family is not allowed to see the body of their daughter before getting it back. Many in the neighbourhood believe they are being overcharged, that she was probably not shot at more than once or twice. Everyone hopes this is the case because, for a family seeing their child for the very last time, even one less bullet hole in their body matters. It matters a lot.

I call several people, and we manage to collect the money needed for one bullet. The rest is put together by the owner of the shop where the woman worked, as well as the neighbours. This is how life is these days. The whole neighbourhood gets together to pay for the bullets inside one person's corpse. Or sometimes it is the whole city.

When the family of the young woman get her body back, they discover that, unfortunately, they were not lied to about the number of bullets.

All night long, I keep wondering whether, when we pay for these bullets, do we, too, become complicit with the regime, providing the money for future bullet replenishments, future murders? Does the Islamic Republic turn every surviving family into its partner in the future murder of citizens?

But who among the survivors is willing to let the body of their loved one be disposed of in the desert by the regime?

I find refuge in the streets, among the people. I take the metro with no destination. I float through the city like a dream whose dreamer has died. Between stations, people just stare at their own reflection in the carriage windows. No words are exchanged. Total silence. Like God's reaction to their suffering.

In taxis, shops or doctors' waiting rooms, I occasionally notice someone crying noiselessly next to me. There is a painful comfort in knowing that other people understand why you are crying: it is a kind of unity in itself.

By the side of the streets, lines of soldiers drain cans of Coca-Cola. Like pilgrims pausing on their way to a shrine, they sit on street corners, eating food out of disposable containers. One time, I deliberately stop and watch them. They hang their helmets from the bushes lining the pavement, pull their sleeves up, tuck white plastic spoons in the containers, shovel heaps of rice and stew into their mouths. One of them shouts at me: 'What are you looking at?' He uses his spoon to signal to me that I need to get going – going on my way, into the void of history. What did Beckett say? 'These creatures have never been, only I and this black void have ever been.'[23]

We have started questioning our past selves. On social media platforms, which we can reach only by using VPNs to circumvent internet censorship, we write about hypocrisies that we have only recently woken up to. How is it that before, we, the women, did not even ask ourselves how a being who has half the rights of a man can be considered one full person when it comes to the ballot box? Why is she considered whole when it comes to voting, but when it comes to daily life, she is considered a half-person, dull-witted and empty-headed?

Dominance over the bodies of women – the perfect examples of marginalised citizens – has been accompanied by dominance over other marginalised groups of society. But it's not only the marginalised who are dominated. The more time passes since the Islamic Revolution of 1979, the more men realise that, even though they have proprietary rights over their wives, daughters and sisters, they will never have full rights to their own bodies. The regime can have them beaten, detained or killed at will. This issue has united men with women and other gender communities, creating a unity that is unprecedented in the history of Islamic patriarchy and its adherents.

This unity began to form in 2009, and it has reached its peak with the Woman, Life, Freedom movement, marking our greatest-yet psychological, social and cultural revolution. It is a unity that is the product of profound rupture. For over a decade, economists have warned about the cracks in our currency's value, and sociologists have evoked various fissures between mainstream society and its cultural norms, with the greatest rupture happening between the Iranian people and the Islam of the Islamic Republic.

Religious dissidents of the Islamic Republic, both inside and outside Iran, have written that no other regime could have done a better job discrediting Islam in the eyes of its followers.

Historians will one day write that, long before losing the war against disbelievers, the Islamic Republic was defeated by devout Muslims who preferred to separate their Islam from that of the Islamic Republic. Their main point of difference is obligation.[24] By not allowing people to choose how they express their faith, the Islamic Republic has revealed itself to be merely a Muslim-branded militia basking in corrupt money, arming itself with helmets and batons. Older generations have been alienated from their Islam, and the new generation is declaring their independence from it – marking the largest loss of Muslim believers in the history of Iran.

This decoupling of personal faith and State has destabilised the government and, like all totalitarian regimes in such circumstances, the Islamic Republic has responded by morphing into its most horrifying form. The monster that was unleashed among the burned-out brothels on that dark night of 1979 has continued to grow and to harass us, fed by more than a thousand years of despotism.

Since the protests started, many of us have assumed that the increasingly choppy quality of the internet is because the regime does not want a high-definition film of its massacre to be broadcast around the world.

But the internet has never been completely shut down this past year. It keeps disconnecting and connecting. The speed diminishes almost to nothing, before getting faster again after a few hours. VPNs are shut down, but new ones soon replace them. All this is not to stop us from accessing information or sharing it; it is to manipulate the *how* of it all. The way we receive news, with delays and in fragments, undermines our sanity more than a total ban ever could.

In the morning, I read in the news that someone has been killed and their body confiscated. Then the internet gets shut down, and I am left struggling with words, images and a boundless imagination that makes me feel I am on the verge of setting my own mind on fire.

In the early or late afternoon, the internet gets connected again. I see videos and pictures from the very moment that person was killed, or snippets from their personal life shared by their loved ones. They are dancing at their birthday party. They are singing. They are making pizza in their kitchen.

At night, if I am lucky enough to access a new, functioning VPN, I learn that the Islamic Republic officers have secretly buried that person, making the traces of violence left on their body disappear beneath the earth, like so many other witnesses of past centuries.

Which one has a more aggressive impact: learning what has happened all at once, or accessing the news in several episodes?

The *drip, drip, drip* of receiving information like this is a form of torture.

It is easy to explain how the three words 'Woman, Life, Freedom' undermine the religious teachings of more than a thousand years. How the words unite all layers of Iranian society, across the spectrum of gender, class and culture, in a revolutionary uprising. How they force the regime, after years of glorying in its victory over the public, to face a frightening array of insurrections led by the very people it once cast out.[25]

By placing ourselves in the shoes of the Islamic Republic, we can easily understand the effort it has devoted to cracking down on us, imprisoning us, executing us. But we keep coming, like waves rising one after another.

In the first days of the movement, it was only women whom the regime nailed to the gates of the city to make examples of. Then followed the LGBTQ+ community, threatened with execution. Later still, long queues formed of writers, labourers and other professions in between; the regime has tried hard to suppress their every protest, upon the pretext that they are threatening public order. The regime did not imagine that medical doctors and lawyers would so quickly also join the movement. Of course, there are also the families of the killed and the political prisoners. And when the regime turns its head, it sees emigrants and exiles outside the borders of Iran shouting slogans against it. The Woman, Life, Freedom movement has become a deluge, the battering of waves on the Islamic Republic's head.

The slogan has become the people's lifeline – a salvation that, rather than coming from Islamic teachings, as the Quran says it should, has appeared from elsewhere and become a noose for those very religious teachings. The three words have also resonated with civil movements in Afghanistan, Syria, Iraq, Germany, France, Israel, the USA, Chile, Argentina and many other countries around the world – with everyone whose life is still held captive under the shadow of patriarchy.

Despite the vast extent of the movement, it still took our parents a while to enter the scene – at least a month or even two. I am sorry to say that some of them have not done so at all. They felt offended when they learned that we named them 'the grey class'. From day one, they have seen the protests as doomed to fail for two reasons – reasons that strike me more as long-standing illusions, the very same reasons that have always helped them avoid confrontations with the regime.

First: they believe the regime in Iran won't change until the West decides it should. 'The West', in this case, means specific countries: the UK, the USA and Israel, and only then other countries. It's a puppet-like way of bringing to power the regimes of the Middle East, this cursed region that claims to be the sworn enemy of the West.

Iranians' belief that we do not have any role in shaping our destiny derives from episodes in our collective memory that cannot be disregarded. Unfortunately, there are many terrible incidents that perfectly illustrate it. The most familiar one is perhaps the 1953 coup d'état – or, as its code name calls it, 'Operation Ajax', during which the US government stirred chaos in Iran, then allocated CIA and MI6 budgets to support Mohammad Reza Shah of Pahlavi to stage a coup against Mosaddegh and the Iranian government, obeying the desires and orders of the USA and the UK.

Another historical mystery that has once again become a source of curiosity and has been discussed during the movement is that of Dorian McGray, an American woman who is said to have travelled from France to Tehran with Khomeini when he first returned to Iran in 1979. In some pictures, she is seen standing right by him, wearing a hijab. She is said to have had a daughter with one of the revolutionary clerics, whom only a few knew about. It is said that she had a lot of power in Khomeini's household, was the only person Khomeini listened to. Some believe she was a CIA spy. Eventually, she just disappeared like a drop of blood on dry earth, with no trace of her whatsoever.

'They themselves brought the mullahs' is a sentence every Iranian has heard uttered many times in their household, and 'they' means none other than the Western governments. When Western countries condemned the regime's actions after the first killings of protestors in 2022 by the Islamic Republic, many of our parents considered their short public statements nothing but mere gestures to keep face. That's why with the publication of the news of the West having secret negotiations with the Islamic Republic regime, the so-called 'grey class' has added yet another proof to their old narrative.

After all, in every point in history, a nation that finds itself defeated prefers to know the causes of its misfortune. It wants to convince itself that it has read the hand of its vanquishers, understands their secrets, knows them all too well. It is only through showcasing its omniscience that it can somehow restore its trampled self-respect.

The second thing that stops our parents' generation from joining the movement is their distrust of our overseas dissidents. An opposition force has formed in the diaspora over the decades, but it has lacked vision in its fight against the Islamic Republic. Especially in the past few months, it has failed to come up with plans to deter the regime's crackdown, to help sustain the movement inside Iran or to usher it to finally toppling the regime. All this has led many people inside the country to wonder about these groups' real motives and whether they derive some ulterior benefit from their demonstrations.

Scrutinising the opposition is important. How can we evaluate the validity of opposition groups if we can't ask about their financial ties, their publicity campaigns or their links to different institutions of power? One crack in our current movement originates from people starting to ask questions about these groups and their leaders, and their questions being met with backlash.

I believe this is one of those moments of reflection that every uprising needs. The movement's exhilarating race towards freedom needs to pause for a second and examine itself, to remove the burden of unrealistic expectation that can end up harming any revolution.

Fracturing the opposition is the grand ploy of totalitarian states, but it has never sufficed to keep them in power.

The regime does not try to hide or even deny the violence it commits against protestors. The same way the Islamic Republic produces 'national products' by circumventing sanctions and importing bits and pieces, it produces local versions of already-tested torture methods imported from all over. It has sent some protestors to mental health hospitals. It has, in the streets, in broad daylight, injected air into the veins of several protestors. It has injected drugs into the blood of many imprisoned protestors, who ended up dying a day or two after their release.

As someone who was born after the 1979 Revolution, who grew up under the Iran–Iraq War, I have many times witnessed the ideological executions of the era I have lived in.

Living through history such as this, being a witness often equals being a criminal. And the punishment for the one who testifies can be martyrdom.

Is it the old fear of bearing witness, and the terror of its consequences, that has led me to delay recounting the end of the story of the high-school girls in the street until now? Is it communal caution that has unconsciously followed me, without me even realising, all the way to this page of the text? Perhaps this holding back is the result of the conservativism drilled into me by my homeland, which, like the exercises for Nastaliq calligraphy, instils discipline.[26]

Or, on the contrary, does it come from wanting to recount everything in detail, to look directly in the eye of censorship and break this age-old bind? Even if I am standing all alone, in the middle of a wild desert of text.

Maybe, up to now, I have been borrowing from the narrative style of our naqqals reciting legends in cafés, building suspense from one scene to the next? Perhaps this is a new *One Thousand and One Nights*?

Actually it's none of the above. I am just trying to follow in the footsteps of our miniaturists: to draw everything down to the smallest details, even the tiny flowers on the pillow of the King, so that you can truly picture our story.

Tahereh

When, during an Islamic Iranian era, after years of teaching her male students through a curtain, Tahereh took off her hijab in front of them, looking them straight in the eye, she did not only demonstrate the backwardness and perverseness of the philosophy behind the hijab. What she insisted on, all the way to the top floor of the chief of police's house and then to the bottom of a well, was to look not only these men, but also their history, in the eye: to stare down the legacy of religious patriarchy in the Middle East.

It took me a while to understand the complex relationship between our history, the era I'm a part of, and my everyday outings.

We are some 20 men and women, walking side by side, not even talking.

And during the autumn and winter of 2022, we walk alongside each other not just through the cities in Iran but through many cities of the world.

Migration and exile have not been strangers to our history. I don't think the diaspora of any land can have been as glorious as ours. Not just because of the glory of our numbers in the streets, but because of our shared understanding of the grandeur of our suffering. Sahifa Banu to India;[27] Mowlana Rumi to Konya; Mahshid Amirshahi, Hedayat and Meskoub to Paris;[28] and millions and millions of other Iranians dispersed around the world. The very people you might have seen in your streets in the past year in large protests, the ones who get on buses in countries around the world to head to one city and join each other for the march – each one of them carries on their shoulders a casket full of unfulfilled wishes for our homeland. Along with a heavy load of guilt for having left.

This shattered diaspora, crying out the name of our homeland in the streets of yours, is speaking about the endurance of a nation throughout wearying centuries. A diaspora standing side by side with those of us who are running in the streets here in Iran.

That afternoon, farther on, I separate from the group of the schoolgirls and once again find myself in one of the streets south of the boulevard. You can simply walk in the streets, and people will join you, and before you know it, you are part of a small group with others who have also come to the street solely to be present here.

This is one of the scenes I look for every day when I leave home while it is still daytime.

The pace of our march is neither fast nor slow. We are relaxed but also ready to run, to escape. It's not today, but only in retrospect, that I understand this moment to be the crux of everything.

A gang of police motorcycles pass behind us in the boulevard, shouting 'Heidar! Heidar!'[29] hysterically and threateningly. In the moment, many of us assume they are headed to the squares south of the boulevard, which tend to be busier.

Their shouts always indicate that something is about to happen. It's like you are standing at the edge of a cursed precipice, about to fall into an endless pit. You sense a coming earthquake, one that will shake to its foundations this city you are marching in, a city where women have been suffocated in wells, been thrown from roofs and been interred beneath buildings.

Before we have walked too far, we suddenly hear screams – a vague and distant buzz that is nonetheless ear-piercing. Nothing is happening in the streets to the south. We are trying to locate the screams when someone shouts that they are coming from Felestin Street. We all run into the first side street.

I have not gone very far when I hear the gunshots: two, one after the other. We keep falling down into the doomed depths. A civilian biker heading in the opposite direction shouts, 'The bastards are shooting people.' We continue to run. And the screams grow louder and louder, echoing more and more heavily off the pavement.

From a distance, I see a few security guards on their motor-cycles, howling, swinging their batons above their heads, bringing them down on whoever is around. I continue to run. The end of the side street keeps coming in and out of focus amid the people's bodies, like pictures taken by the fast, continuous clicks of a camera shutter. Suddenly, several women's unified screams fill the air.

This is one of the grand moments when the rage outside on the streets joins the anxiety inside us, only to guide us towards death. It is the kind of moment you see in famous war photographs, showing a person, all alone and unarmed, standing tall in front of armed guards. No one really knows what the catalyst for these moments is. No one knows what happens in the seconds before the subject of the photograph decides to run towards their death.

This is one aspect of a movement that gets lost on TV screens, in history books and in newspaper pages: the death-driven force of being a witness. Perhaps it is linked to courage, but it is not courage per se. It is a strange combination of heroism and vanity that propels us to run in the streets.[30]

We are running, and only a moment before reaching the main street, I notice the police van leaving. There is no need to rush any more. They have already arrested those they needed.

Soon after the van's departure, the motorcycle roars get closer, and as a finale, the remaining guards and plain-clothes forces hit the protestors with batons to disperse the rest of the crowd. I return to a side street and start running again. Air and blood swirl together in my throat while I look for a refuge between the bodies. I take some big steps, and then ... then, it is as if something passes under my feet, something that looks like a cavity. A small, dark pit.

Through the bodies of others, I pull myself towards the door of a house and look back. I can see it under others' feet: a shapeless mark, the trace of dark-red blood, looking black in the sunset. The remains of the daylight dances over the tarmac but not on the pothole of blood under the corpse of a woman at the bottom of a well.

Did I jump over the mark deliberately or was it just a continuation of the bouncing steps of a person on the run?

I see a small maroon spot on the side of my trainers. Then, I hear the whispers: several high-school girls were hit by batons and taken away; one of them was dragged along the pavement; one of them was shot.

Even the book of our history, overwritten with cruelties, cannot prepare me to face this fresh blood.

The red cosmos on the ground does not date back, like the ones in the skies, to millions of years ago, but to only a few moments ago. In its face, all punishments fall short, grow silent. The punishments and murders I have seen pictures of or read about in the past few decades – the stoning of women, the executions without trials or with sham trials, the tortures, the cutting of veins.

It is only in this silence that I can stand up to announce that I am a witness, and I, hereby, testify.

I will never know whose blood was on the ground, out of all the girls from that group I met. I can only testify to its crimson colour. I can only testify that I have witnessed the soul of a nation cracking.

I am a whole witness. I am present at the scene of the crime. I have been all my life. I, a woman whose testimony is worth half of a man's.

If I leave home during daylight, it is because I want to see everything clearly – even a thing like this. So that I can be a full witness to the era I am living in.

Living can be passive. Witnessing is not passive.

These are the words I want to send into the future, having walked through blood. For those who will come after us and who, in the vortex of our history, will look for us. If they look for us.

Notes

1. Similar to a long overcoat, manteaus became mandatory for women after the 1979 Revolution. A few years before the 2022 demonstrations, some women had already started defying this mandate by wearing shorter jackets or dresses, a choice that could lead to their arrest by the so-called 'morality police'.

2. Vladimir Mayakovsky, 'A Cloud in Trousers', in John Glad and Daniel Weissbort (editors), *Russian Poetry: The Modern Period* (Iowa: University of Iowa Press, 1978).

3. In Islamic law, stoning is a capital punishment for women who commit acts of infidelity.

4. Babism, or the Babi movement, is a post-Islamic religion that was founded by Sayyid 'Ali Muhammad Shirazi, or the Bab, in 19th-century Iran.

5. Fewer than 60 short poems remain from Tahereh; some of these are only attributed to her.

6. The Conference of Badasht, held by leading Babis in June–July 1848.

7. Imam Zaman, Hazrat-e Mahdi, the twelfth imam of Shiite Islam, is the messianic absent imam believed to emerge at the end of time to bring us peace and justice.

8. Naw'i Khabushani, *Suz o Godaz* [*Burning and Melting*]. Naw'i Khabushani was a Persian poet of the 16th and early 17th centuries.

9. Muhammad Taqi Lisan al-Mulk Sipihr, *Nasikh al-Tawarikh*. This is a book on the Qajar era.

10. Tahereh, Qurrat al-Ayn, collection of poems, edited by Hesam Noghabayi.

11. Pahlevan was a title given to noble, courageous wrestlers who were highly regarded not only for their bravery but also because of their manners and care for people.

12. The maghna'eh is a type of head covering that is more formal than an ordinary scarf; it is mandated in schools and public offices by the Islamic Republic regime.

13. Joseph Brodsky, 'Less than One', *New York Review of Books*, September 27, 1979 issue

14. The schools of Iranian miniature include Shiraz, Tabriz, Harat and Isfahan, each with their own characteristics.

15. Persian miniature does not follow the same rules of perspective as Western painting, instead depicting buildings and cities in a flat manner.

16. Men, too, were forced to wear a certain type of hat, while clerics had to remove their turbans and abayas. Some believe these dress codes forced on men gave rise to dissatisfaction with the rule of the Pahlavi King, Reza Shah.

17. There are accounts of many women beaten in the so-called morality police vans and detention centres; their bodies disappeared afterwards. We only know the truth about one of them: Mahsa-Jina Amini.

18. In our tales, there are many depictions of our mystics flying, walking on water or covering long distances in the blink of an eye.

19. The 'Baraye' ('For') song by Shervin Hajipour won the first-ever Best Song for Social Change award in the 65th Annual Grammy Awards.

20. Ignazio Silone, *The School for Dictators* (New York: Atheneum, 1963). Frank Dikötter, *How to Be a Dictator: The Cult of Personality in the Twentieth Century* (New York: Bloomsbury Publishing, 2019). Afsaneh Najmabadi, 'Is Our Name Remembered?: Writing the History of Iranian Constitutionalism as if Women and Gender Mattered', in *Iranian Studies*, 29 1–2 (1996), 85–109. Chimamanda Ngozi Adichie, *We Should All Be Feminists* (London: HarperCollins*Publishers*, 2014).

21. The Chain Murders of Iran were a series of murders and disappearances of Iranian intellectuals and writers who had been critical of the regime. They were carried out between 1988 and 1998 by Islamic Republic agents.

22. Muslims believe the son chosen for sacrifice was Ismael, while in the Bible, he is Isaac.

23. Samuel Beckett, Steven Connor (editor), *The Unnamable* (New York: Grove Press, 1958) [French original, *L'Innommable* (Paris: Les Éditions de Minuit, 1953)].

24. Since the start of the protests, the Iranian people have been accused of Islamophobia by Muslim citizens of other countries. However, it is necessary to remember the difference between compulsory Islam, as in Iran, and Islam practised freely. I wonder why, in the minds of some Muslims, questioning the violence of Islam is considered an insult, even punishable by death? Growing up in the cradle of the Islamic regime, we experience censorship and suffocation doubly: once from the regime and once from the Muslims elsewhere in the world.

25. Of the German student movement of 1960, Sabine Von Dirke writes: 'The socio-cultural uprising of 1960 [...] overcame the boundaries of a subculture and intermingled a lifestyle revolution with new cultural and aesthetic, as well as political desires.' We can, thus, say that the Woman, Life, Freedom movement is such a socio-political movement.

26. Learning Nastaliq calligraphy, a student begins by tracing faint patterns of the letters on the exercise page with their calligraphy pen, much as young kids learn to write the letters of the alphabet.

27. Sahifa Banu was an Iranian painter from the 16th century.

28. Amirshahi, Hedayat and Meskoub are all Iranian writers.

29. 'Heidar' means 'lion', a name given to Imam Ali by Prophet Mohammad.

30. This refers to the themes of heroism in the poetry of Ferdowsi and that of vanity in the poetry of Khayyam.